Union Ghosts

by Susan Crites

Butternut Publications
Martinsburg, West Virginia 25401
1993

Published by
Butternut Publications
P.O. Box 1851
Martinsburg, West Virginia 25401

First printing April 1993

ISBN 1-881562-06-9

Manufactured in the United States of America

10 9 8 7 6 5 4 3 2

DEDICATION

To those fathers, brothers and sons who,
believing in the sanctity of the Union,
went forth to do battle in the great Civil War
and to those who remain there—locked in time.

INTRODUCTION

My mother's family contributed five brothers to the enormous and dreadful Civil War. My great-great-grandfather was among the four brothers who fought for the Confederacy.

We know very little about the one brother who fought for the Union, save only that he was said to have died in battle.

In truth, he survived the war but was considered dead by a passionate Confederate family who couldn't bear to have a traitor to the South among them. He, like so many others, was lost in that shattering epoch in our history. There are many other Union soldiers who were lost in a different way.

The tales of ghosts who haunt the battlefields and the towns between them in the northern Shenandoah Valley are more abundant than flakes of snow in a storm. The first credible sightings of both Union and Confederate ghosts were reported by local residents within days of any battle or skirmish. The ghost sightings have persisted for more than one hundred and thirty years.

For more than a year, I have been interviewing people who believe that they have encountered the supernatural.

Their stories have been as varied as the people who told them. I have spoken with scientists and homemakers; firemen and computer programmers; school teachers and retired military officers.

I've seen compelling evidence of ghosts with a sense of humor, ghosts on a mission of mercy and ghosts with vengeful murder in their hearts.

I've also seen tangible proof of ghosts in the form of photographs, audio and video tape.

I've touched the souvenirs ghosts have left behind with startled and shaken participants in experiences with the supernatural; coins, a horseshoe, a pocket watch, and much more.

I've visited places that seemed normal in every way yet, they felt menacing, eerily cold, or overwhelming sad. Each of my senses has been affected by a sound or a smell that is best described as "other worldly."

The most fascinating ghosts are the spirits who remain from the time of the Civil War.

For four long years, the people of the upper Shenandoah Valley were caught in a hurricane of blood and battle. Armies surged back and forth across the land so frequently that a city like Martinsburg, Shepherdstown or Winchester could be occupied by both armies in a single day!

The people of the upper Shenandoah Valley lived amid the armies. They fed them, laughed with them, conspired against them, nursed them, and buried them.

Tales of Union ghost sightings have been told since the early days of the war. Generation after generation has seen the blue-clad apparitions. They are seen today!

As a result of my experiences in researching the ghosts in this area, I have no doubt whatsoever that Union ghosts exist and that the stories told by the many who have had encounters with them are true.

I was given permission to use these stories of recent encounters with Union ghosts on the condition that the contributors remain anonymous. I have presented these stories as closely as possible to the way I heard them. I have changed nothing.

Ghosts are not the product of an overactive imagination or the imaginings of a lunatic. They aren't even the experience of strangers.

Ghosts haunt our friends and neighbors; people we trust. They appear in your town. They are seen, quite literally, every day, somewhere near the place where you are reading these words.

Perhaps, you will be the next to encounter the supernatural!

Susan Crites
Martinsburg, West Virginia

CONTENTS

THE LANTERN

Author's Note: The land surrounding Berryville, Virginia is picturesque. The homes and farms blend with the landscape to make a timeless picture of a majestic and bountiful land.

I met them at their home located just a few miles from Winchester. We sat on the porch sipping lemonade.

They are a recently retired couple who moved to Virginia from Texas to be close to their children. She is learning to weave and he is pursuing a long-held dream of building fine furniture. This is what they told me.

Moving "back east" was not an easy decision for us. We are accustomed to the wide spaces and big skies. Things are just a little too cramped in the east for most Westerners. In the end, Mother, here, wanted to be near the children and so we moved.

The children are in the suburbs of Washington; one is in Arlington and the other is in Manassas. Berryville is short ride for them, by Texas standards, and there's enough space here to have a little breathing room for us.

This property was once a thriving farm with a house, a couple of barns and assorted outbuildings. By the time we bought it, the only thing left standing was a dilapidated old chicken coop. Even after years of disuse, you can always smell the chickens!

We had this house built along with the barn and two cinder block buildings. I wanted a shop and Mother wanted a place for her loom. Since the construction didn't cost near as much as we had planned, I had the chicken coop fixed up. I guess it was a darn fool thing to do but we decided to preserve a little history — such as it was.

We moved into the new spread and hunkered down into a peaceful retirement. The kids came to visit frequently, Mother enjoyed her weaving, and I was making the kind of furniture I'd dreamed about for so long.

One night I was out in my shop and I heard a ruckus coming from the chicken coop. I need to tell you that we may have fixed it up but we surely didn't put any chickens in it. The ruckus I heard was chickens squawking. Couldn't believe my ears!

I grabbed my flashlight because it gets mighty dark in these parts and I walked toward the coop.

I hadn't gotten five feet out of the door of my shop when someone shot at me. I'd been in my share of fire fights during my stint in the Marine Corps. I dropped the flashlight and hit the dirt in a heckuva hurry.

Bullets kept zinging and chickens were flappin'. I couldn't imagine what was going on. I decided to make tracks toward the house and ran in crouch toward it. The gunfire kept up.

I ran up the steps and across the porch faster'n jack rabbit getting away from a hungry coyote and dove through the front door, slamming it shut behind me.

Mother was crouched behind the sofa and said, "My God, William, it sounds like a war out there!"

I ran for the rifle cabinet, unlocked it, grabbed for my shotgun and box of shells. As I was getting Mother safely into the kitchen, the glass shattered in the front window. I could hear horses and men shouting.

I crept toward the broken window and stole a peek outside. There were men in uniform all around the house. They were shooting at my shop and the chicken coop.

A voice rang out from one of the horsemen. "You folks in there stay down! We'll get them Rebel stragglers."

I watched in utter amazement as blue-clad cavalrymen sent a withering volley of fire into that coop. They shot it to pieces. I could hear shouting, screams, the creak of leather and the clanking of metal against metal. It was bedlam.

Suddenly, the firing and hullabaloo stopped.

I waited with my head down for what seemed like eternity. Finally, I heard Mother come up softly behind me. She said she thought it was over.

I looked outside cautiously, I couldn't see a soul. With my gun at ready, I flipped on the spotlights that illuminated the path from the house to the out buildings and opened the front door.

I could see that the yard was a mess. The grass was torn up; covered with tracks and horse flop. The coop was demolished and there were these scrawny dead chickens clearly visible in the debris.

Mother and I were flat bewildered by it all. Without a word, we went inside, poured ourselves a stiff drink, and I called the local police to let them know we'd had a little problem.

About half an hour later, the police arrived. I could see their cruiser lights flashing as they came up the drive and went out to meet them with Mother right behind me.

Just as the officers were opening the doors of the cruiser, I think Mother and I saw, at just about the same time, that it was all gone; the chicken coop was back to normal, the grass had no hoof marks, there were no bullet holes.

When the officers got up to the porch and asked about our problem, I mumbled something about odd noises. Mother was speechless.

They took a look around the property and returned a few minutes later with an old lantern. I'd never seen it before but they said they had found it just sitting on the ground, over by my shop. It was still burning and they told me to be careful because it could start a fire.

I never did find my flashlight.

Author's Note: They decided to tear the chicken coop down and I saw only where it once stood. The other buildings showed no signs of damage.

I saw the old lantern. The folks from Texas had taken it to a railroad history expert in Washington, D.C. He provided them with an exhaustive analysis.

There were three initials and a date scratched onto the bottom of the lantern. They were MGR 62. The expert said that the lantern was authentic and was consistent with those used by trainmen on the the Manassas Gap Railroad. In 1862, that railroad was in the hands of the Confederate army.

Stragglers or men from both sides who fell behind the march of their armies were a problem for civilians and armies alike. Separated from their units, they often behaved as heavily armed thieves. Whenever possible, soldiers tried to protect civilians from their depredations.

THE APPLE TREE

Author's Note: He is twenty-five years old with a muscular build. He graduated from Martinsburg High School and drives a truck. I talked with him in a coffee shop in Morgan County, West Virginia. He seemed very nervous. This is what he said.

I'd just gotten paid and decided to visit a little honky-tonk just over the Jefferson County line. I spent a few hours drinkin' cold brew and laughin' with the boys.

About midnight, I decided it was time to hang it up and headed for my truck. I got a few miles down the road and knew I'd better pull off, catch a few winks. If the "man" happened to pull me over, I was in no shape to walk the line.

I pulled my pick up onto a dirt road and parked it two or three miles down in the thick of some apple trees. I pushed my cap over my eyes and fell out.

Next thing I knew, I heard someone beatin' on my truck. I sat up, pushed my hat back and focused my eyes on some big dude on a horse, standing right by the truck.

Whang! He hit the rear view mirror on the door. I was mad and told him none too nicely that he better back off right quick. Whang! He hit the door again and said something stupid like, “Show yourself, Reb.”

By this time, I knew I was dealing with a nut case. I reached over and jerked my gun out from under the seat, threw the door open, and jumped out. I brought my arm up to put the gun on him and I felt a pain, like lightning; in my wrist. It shot clear up to my shoulder. The crazy man on the horse had knocked the gun out of my hand with the flat of a sword. I'm not kidding you, it was a sword.

When he told me to put my hands up over my head, I'll tell you, I did it in a New York minute. A crazy man on a horse with a sword is nothin' to fool with.

When he asked me what I was doin' out in the orchard, I gave him my best smile, shrugged and admitted I'd had too much to drink.

He sent a chill through me when he said, with the coldest voice I've ever heard, that I was a rebel spy and that there was too much of that among the people of Martinsburg.

The moon was bright and I got a good look at that man. He was dressed in a blue uniform, all right. He was armed to the teeth with that sword, a big pistol in a flap holster, and a short rifle that hung from his hip. He looked tough!

He kept staring a big hole through me. When his right hand started to move toward that flap holster, I took off runnin' like my life depended on it. There was no doubt in my mind that it did, for real!

I dodged between them trees and that crazy man chased me so bad I thought I could feel that horse's breath on my neck.

I was runnin' out of steam after a while and ran behind the biggest tree I could find. I stood there terrified and heavin' for air when he came at me, bent down low. He swung that sword at my head and I threw myself backwards to get out of the way. I think I hit my head on a rock when I connected with the ground. I thought I heard a loud "thunk" of that sword hitting the tree just before I blacked out.

I woke up in the sunlight. I was a surprised man to still be alive. My head hurt and my mouth was like cotton.

It took me a while to stand up but, when I did, the first thing I saw was this old sword sticking through the tree right beside me. That sword hadn't been shoved through that apple tree, either. The tree was growing around it!

Author's Note: He went back and cut down the tree, carefully preserving two feet of trunk above and below the sword. He keeps it in a closet in his trailer and hasn't told his friends or family about his encounter.

The sword embedded in the tree trunk is a Union army, cavalry-issue, M1860 light saber. It has a brass hilt with three branches topped with a Phrigian helmet pommel. It is 34 5/8 inches long. It was a traditional cavalrymen's weapon during the Civil War.

Among the citizens of Martinsburg during the Civil War, there were many passionate Confederate sympathizers. They conspired against the Union armies at every opportunity. Some, like the famous Belle Boyd, were defiant of the Union soldiers. They devoted considerable energy to gathering and delivering information about their enemy.

THE DOLL

Author's Note: She lives near the historic district in Winchester, Virginia. She is 89 years old. She had sixteen relatives who fought in the Civil War; all of them died in battle or of disease or in a cruel Northern prison camp. She is a small woman who dresses with understated elegance. This is her remarkable story.

I was born just after the turn of the century and grew up on a small farm a mile or so off of what we now call Route 11, south of Winchester.

We lost my grandfather early in the Great War, the War Between The States. We lost all older his brothers and their sons, too. When I came along that war had been over for nearly forty years but it was fresh in the minds of the women who lived through it.

My first and most treasured possession is this doll. It isn't much; a few bits of cloth and wooden-button eyes but, the oldest woman in my family, Aunt Eleanor, put it in my arms just days after my birth. The doll's name is "My." For as long as anyone can remember, Aunt Eleanor has told me to tell everyone and anyone who would listen that this is "My Doll."

There's always been a lot of talk and stories in the family about the War. Folks can't seem to forget it. When I was very small I began to have dreams about the War. When I talked about my dreams, it seemed natural to everyone that I might dream about the dramatic things I had heard from others.

When I was about six, I took My and went to play in the attic on a rainy day. I remember looking in crates and dusty trunks for a short while. Then I decided to lift up a floor board under the biggest trunk. No one ever told me about that floor board but I knew it was there. Naturally, I was too little to move that big trunk so, I ran down the stairs and begged one of my bothers to move it for me. The boys always indulged me and the trunk was moved.

I lifted up that floor board and found a package containing a little torn, soiled dress and several gold coins. I put the package back carefully, pushed some boxes over the spot and I didn't say anything to anyone.

That night, I had my first dream of a golden-haired girl with blue eyes and dimples. She was left-handed. In my dream, we played together in the big oak tree behind the house. It was such a happy dream.

The next morning at the breakfast table, out of the clear blue, I asked Momma why my great uncle

John had died from an infection in his big toe. She dropped a plate and broke it. She whipped around and asked me who had told me he died from an infection. I said I couldn't remember. She walked over to me, and shook me a little saying that Uncle John died in battle not from an infection. Her intensity scared me and I swore I'd never say it again.

Over the years, I had my dream of playing with the blonde, blue-eyed girl many times. When I was about thirteen, I went to town with my Aunt Eleanor. We were some place on Braddock Street when I asked her what became of the Mercantile with all the candy I liked so well. She patted my hand and said that it was long gone.

The next day, she took me all by myself on a picnic. We had chicken, lemonade, and all the fixins. It was a wonderful afternoon. After we finished eating, she took my hands in hers and talked to me ever so kindly.

She asked me if I was aware that I knew many more things than a girl my age should know. I didn't quite understand what she meant so, she asked me if I remembered talking about how Uncle John had died. I said yes. Then she told me that his death was a family secret; that John had shot himself in the foot to avoid fighting in a battle. The family hid his cowardice in a story that he died in the battle and no one, absolutely no one, ever mentioned to death from infection.

"How did I find out?" I asked.

"Your doll, My helps you." she said. "You have a very special gift, child. I've always known about you. I hope that soon you'll know about yourself."

I didn't understand that conversation with my aunt. I knew she was right, though. I always seemed to know more about the men who died in the war than the other children. I even knew silly things like when the wooden floor was put into the kitchen or what the weather was like when the family got the news about Appomattox. All of that was before I was born but somehow I knew.

That night, I took My to bed and had nightmares. The little blond girl and I were playing near the house. She suggested that we play with the hoop and stick in the road. I told her we weren't allowed to play in the road. All night long she begged me to go with her to play in the road. Finally, I agreed.

As we approached the road, we saw these Yankees walking past the house. Their lines went on for hours. When we saw the last of them, we took the big metal hoop into the road and rolled it. The point of the game was to see who could make it roll the longest distance before it fell over.

It was her turn and she was tapping the hoop, skipping behind it when I saw Yankees in wagons tearing down the road toward us. I called to her and warned her to get out the way. She seemed not to hear me.

I stood there in horror as a fast-moving wagon bore down on her. I cried out for her to jump away. Just as the wagon was about to hit her, the Yankee with all the reins pulled them hard to the right, trying to avoid the little girl but it was too late. She fell under the wheels, life rushed out of her.

I awoke from that dream screaming, shaking and crying. Finally, Momma put My into my arms to quiet me. When I touched the doll, I knew I was that little blonde girl who died so young and was given another chance at life.

Author's Note: She showed me an old letter written with a shaky hand. It was from her Aunt Eleanor dated February 3, 1921. It said,

> *"My dear child,*
>
> *On the day that your cousin, Ada, was killed, she appeared to me. In life, I loved her as my own. Her death, after so many in the war, was a devastation to me. She told me there was no need to be sad because she would be back in my lifetime. She said that heaven was*

too full of those who had died in the war and she wasn't needed. She kissed me, looked at me with those wonderful blue eyes and said, 'Save my doll.' Then she disappeared.

When you were born, I knew that you were my dear Ada returning to me. Your mother knew as well. Your first word was my name.

The torn dress you found so long ago was Ada's, worn the day she died. The gold coins were from the soldier who drove the wagon.

You have been given an extraordinary gift of two lives. Upon my death, you will inherit all that I own. Use it to make the most of your remarkable life."

For sixty years, she has collected information about and artifacts from the Union troops who served in the Winchester area. She hopes to identify the soldier who caused Ada's death—before her own.

THE GARDEN

Author's Note: We sat in their spacious yard behind a modest home of modern construction just outside of Williamsport, Maryland. The most commanding feature of the yard is a finely landscaped and maintained rock garden. The garden is more than 100 feet long and twenty feet wide.

He works for a large corporation in Hagerstown, Maryland and she is a home maker. They have three riotous little girls who seem to be in constant motion. This is their story.

We bought this land for a song back in the early Seventies. There was an old house still standing on it but we had it torn down. We placed this house on the old foundation and saved ourselves a few bucks.

We've got about an acre behind the house. We wanted a big yard for the kids with a play house, sand box, swings and so forth. The children in our family tend to be very high-spirited. A big, fenced yard is the best place for them to use up all that energy they inherited.

After the house was built, we went to work on developing an even, grassy yard. The land was lumpy, full of sudden depressions and unexpected humps. It was easy to twist an ankle out there. It was a patchwork quilt of weeds and bare spots.

My husband hired a man to bring in a tractor with a disk to break up the earth and even things out a little. He worked for a day, finishing half the yard, and quit. He complained that he was hitting too many buried rocks and that he would ruin his equipment if he continued.

Having become quite familiar with some of the local price gouging practices during the construction of our home, I didn't offer him a financial incentive to continue. I paid him and sent him on his merry way.

The next day, after my husband went to work and I took the children to pre-school and kindergarten, I put on my work clothes and went to the yard.

I walked the section that had been broken up and to look for the odious rocks. I was astonished to see hundreds of what looked like small pieces of bone about the size of my thumb.

I returned to the house, put on my gloves, picked up a plastic pan, and returned to the yard to collect the white-grey things. In less than an hour, I had a tub of them and was tired. I took them into the house, put them on the table and drank a glass of tea.

While I was resting, I looked at my tub and realized that I had been collecting bullets. They looked like something I had seen years before on a class trip to Gettysburg National Battlefield.

When my husband came home, I showed him the tub and he was excited. He said we might be the proud owners of a civil war battle or skirmish site. He said he would check with someone in the history department at the local college as soon as possible.

That night, the children were fussy. They wouldn't eat their dinner, take a bath or go to sleep without the light. I couldn't imagine what was wrong with them.

About four in the morning, one of the girls screamed. We ran up to her room, flicked on the light and saw that she was terrified. We rushed to comfort her and she began to cry that there was a monster in the yard. Nothing we could do would comfort her so, we carried her to bed with us. Soon, she went to sleep and we whispered to one another, wondering what could have frightened her.

An hour later, we were awakened by the younger girls. They ran into our bedroom shrieking that a monster was in the yard and we would all die.

I held the children while my husband picked up the only weapon in the house, a golf club, and went to investigate the yard. When he returned, he was ashen but, for the girl's sake, he said there vas nothing.

In time, the children went back to sleep in our bed as we sat with near them. When I was sure they were sound asleep, I asked him what he had seen.

He said the earth on the side of the yard that hadn't been tilled had popped up. I looked at him quizzically and he said very softly that two graves had appeared in our back yard.

Suddenly, I was frightened. I insisted that we dress the children and go to a nearby motel. In less than fifteen minutes, we were out of there!

The next day, my husband called two of his burliest friends, explained the situation and asked for their help in discovering what was going on in the yard. I waited with the children while he met his friends at our house.

My husband was gone for more than eight hours. He called periodically to say that they had found something but he was quite safe. He also said we would be spending several nights at the motel.

When he returned, we left the children with a friend of mine who had joined me in my vigil at the motel. She agreed to watch the children while we slipped away for dinner and a chance to talk.

I wasn't prepared for what he told me. They went to the house expecting to find two graves but found seven. He said that the men spent the day excavating the graves and the area around them. Digging was difficult because each man swore that, from time to time, he felt the ground moving under his feet.

Even more astonishing was his calm declaration that each grave contained a Union soldier in a uniform that was perfectly preserved; no dry rot, no worm holes, no deterioration of any kind.

I promptly declared that I would never take my babies back to that place. My husband reluctantly agreed. The whole thing was very bizarre.

That night, both my husband and I were restless. We both had vivid yet peculiar dreams. I awakened with a start and saw him standing at the foot of the bed drenched in sweat. The children, thank heaven, were in a deep sleep.

We washed our faces and climbed back into bed. We were both exhausted. I began to tell him what I had dreamed. I had been in battle. It was a chaos of explosion, gunfire, screams and smoke. There were men in light brown uniforms all around me. I could feel the bullets enter my body. I was dying. My friends around me were falling and dying. I wanted a place to rest.

My husband touched my arm. His hands were cold and trembling. He said he had the same dream, exact in every detail. In that moment of revelation, we both fell asleep again. When we awakened, we were both calm and returned to the house.

Author's Note: They buried the soldiers in carefully prepared graves. Their burial was attended by a few close friends who participated in a memorial service. Over their graves they constructed the wonderful rock garden, a beautiful place to rest. Since that time, there have been no monsters to frighten the children.

In July 1863, a short but wild battle took place near Williamsport, Maryland between Confederate defenders of an ambulance train retreating from the battle of Gettysburg and Union troops under the command of General John Buford. Federal losses in the battle were 72 men. During a hasty Union retreat, all the dead were left behind. Records of their burials are sketchy.

ABOUT THE AUTHOR

Susan Crites, a seventh-generation West Virginian, is the author of several best-selling books set in West Virginia, and has been one of its most popular writers. Her thrilling yet wholesome style continues to earn Crites an enthusiastic national following. She resides in Martinsburg, West Virginia, where she writes about the people and land she loves.

Other Books By Susan Crites

Lively Ghosts of the
Eastern Panhandle of West Virginia
A chilling collection of contemporary ghost stories told by West Virginia friends and neighbors
____0-681-87305-1/$5.00

Strange and Amusing Tales of the
Eastern Panhandle of West Virginia
A delightfully entertaining glimpse of the unique culture and humor of West Virginia
____0-681-87307-8/$5.00

Murder in Martinsburg
Join Samantha, Denver and the lovable cat Foghorn, as the most delightful detective team in West Virginia sets out to solve the mystery and find a murderer
____1-881-56200-x/$10.00

More Lively Ghosts
More true, never before published ghost stories from Maryland, Pennsylvania, Virginia and West Virginia
____1-881-56201-8/$5.00

PLEASE SEND THE TITLES CHECKED ABOVE
MAIL ORDERS TO:
Butternut Publications
P.O. Box 1851
Martinsburg, WV 25401

Name: ______________________________

Address: ______________________________

City: ______________________________

State: ____________________ Zip: ____________

TOTAL BOOKS: ____________

PLUS $1.00 POSTAGE and HANDLING: ____________

TOTAL ORDER: ____________

prices subject to change

COMING SOON!

MURDER AT CONFEDERATE HEADQUARTERS

by
Susan Crites

When an alert researcher finds a vague reference to the murder of a junior officer assigned to a Confederate General's Berkeley County Headquarters, the Civil War Society launches an effort to solve the century-old crime.

When they discover that the crime is remarkably similar to several recent murders in Berkeley County, they wonder if they have discovered a killer from another time.

Join Samatha Carter, Denver Casto and the lovable cat Foghorn, as the most delightful detective team in West Virginia sets out to solve the mystery and find a murderer!

Murder at Confederate Headquarters
Another exciting adventure
by West Virginia author
Susan Crites

During the Civil War artists produced drawings in the field which were sent back to their offices to be redrawn on hardwood blocks and printed as line-cuts. Within several weeks of any event, illustrations by artists who were there could be seen throughout the country. The background cover art of ***Union Ghosts*** appeared in the weekly tabloid size publication, *Harpers Weekly* in 1862. It depicts a cavalry battle in the Eastern Theater.